A Hou

MW00657274

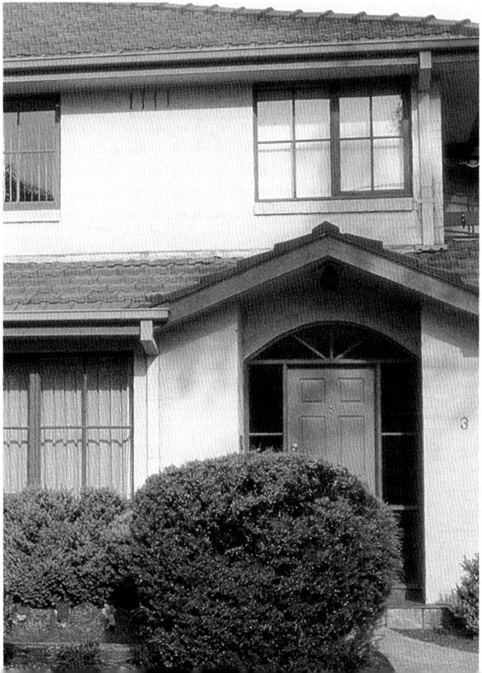

Here is a gate.

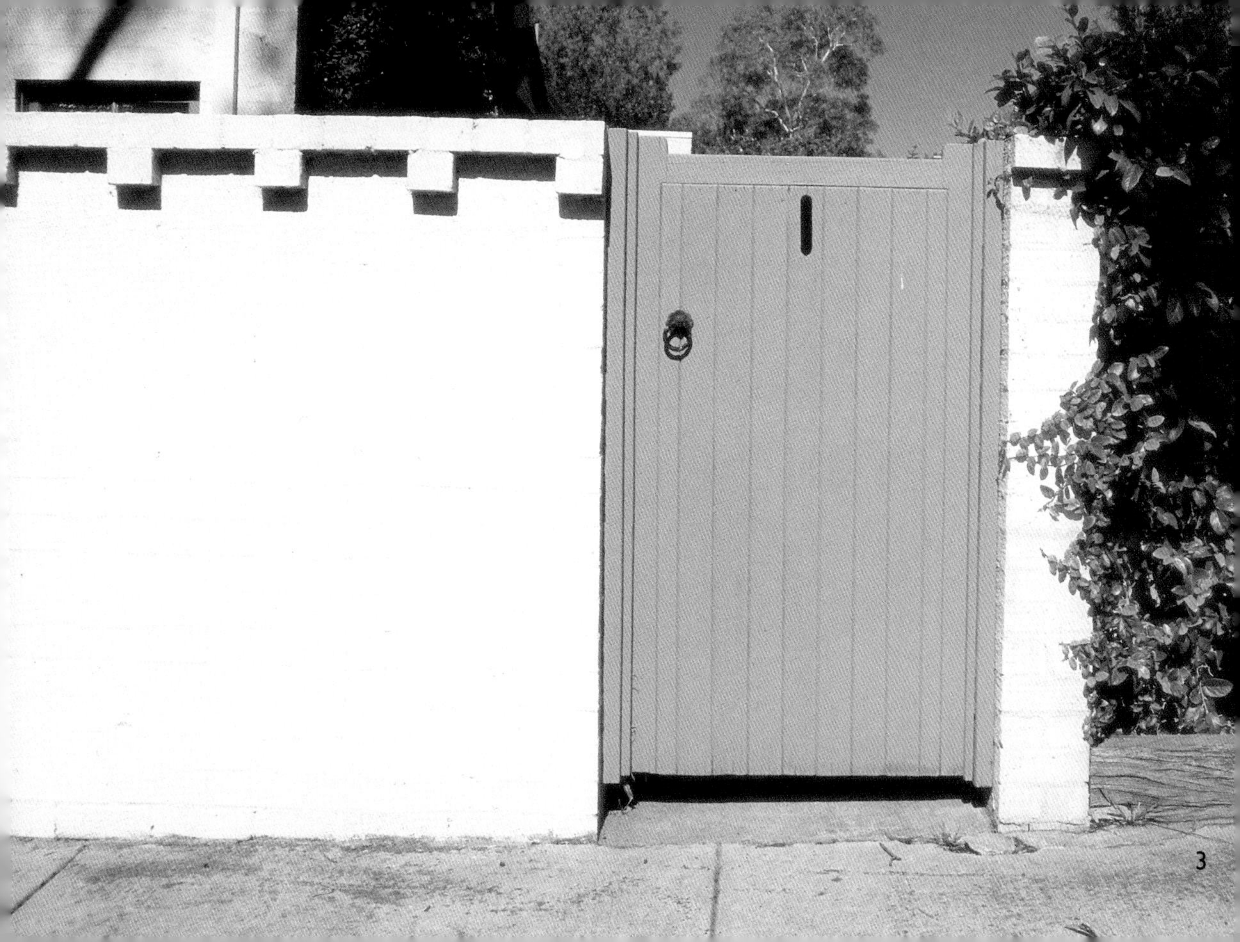

Here is a path.

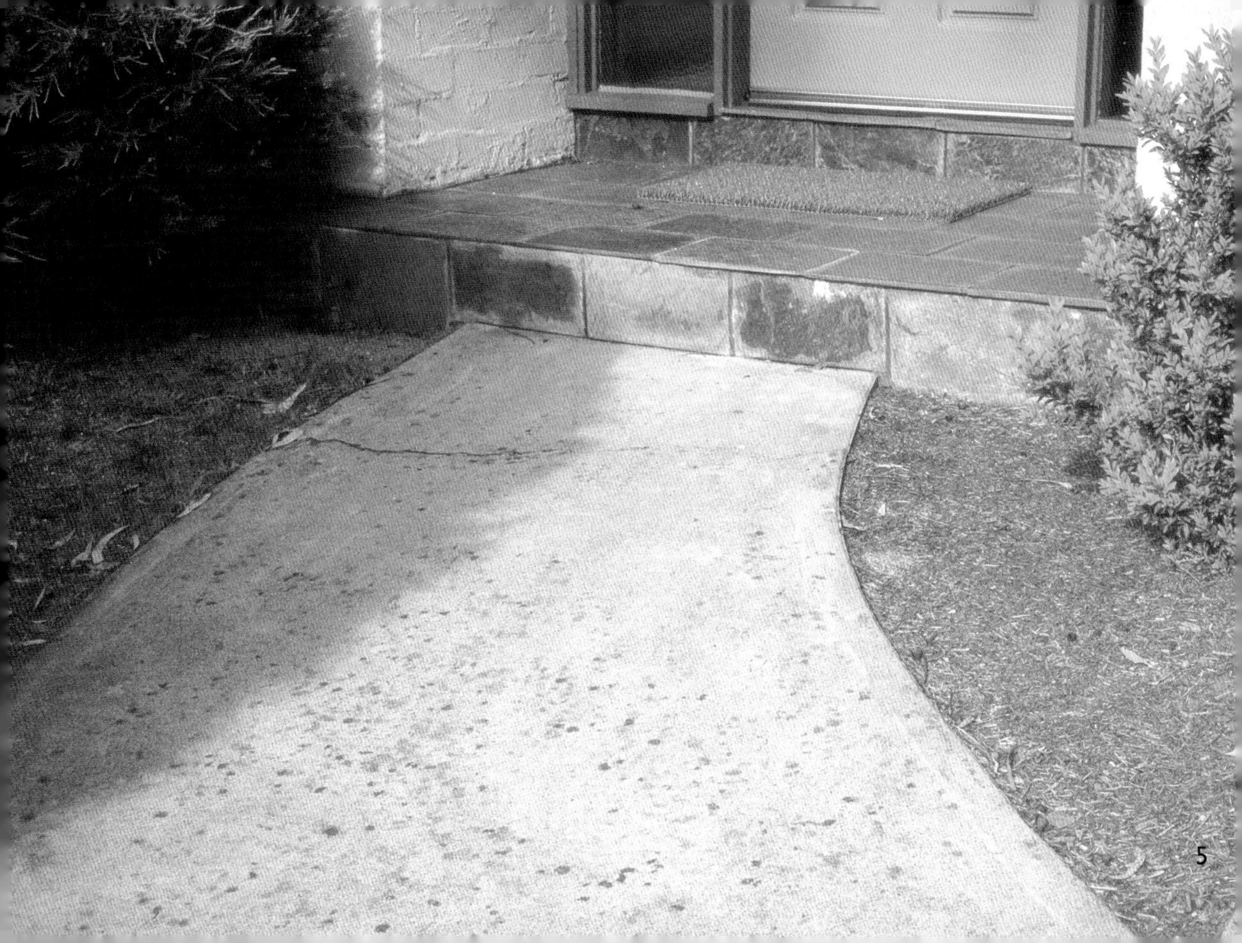

Here is a door.

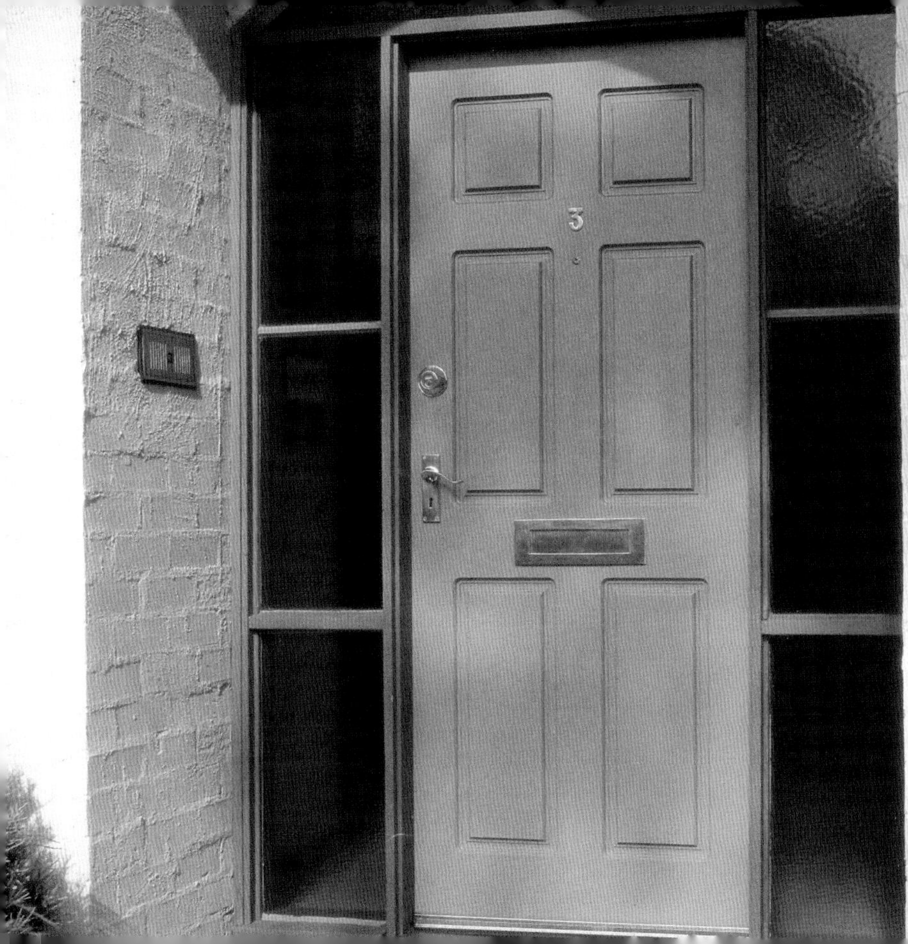
3
3

Here is a window.

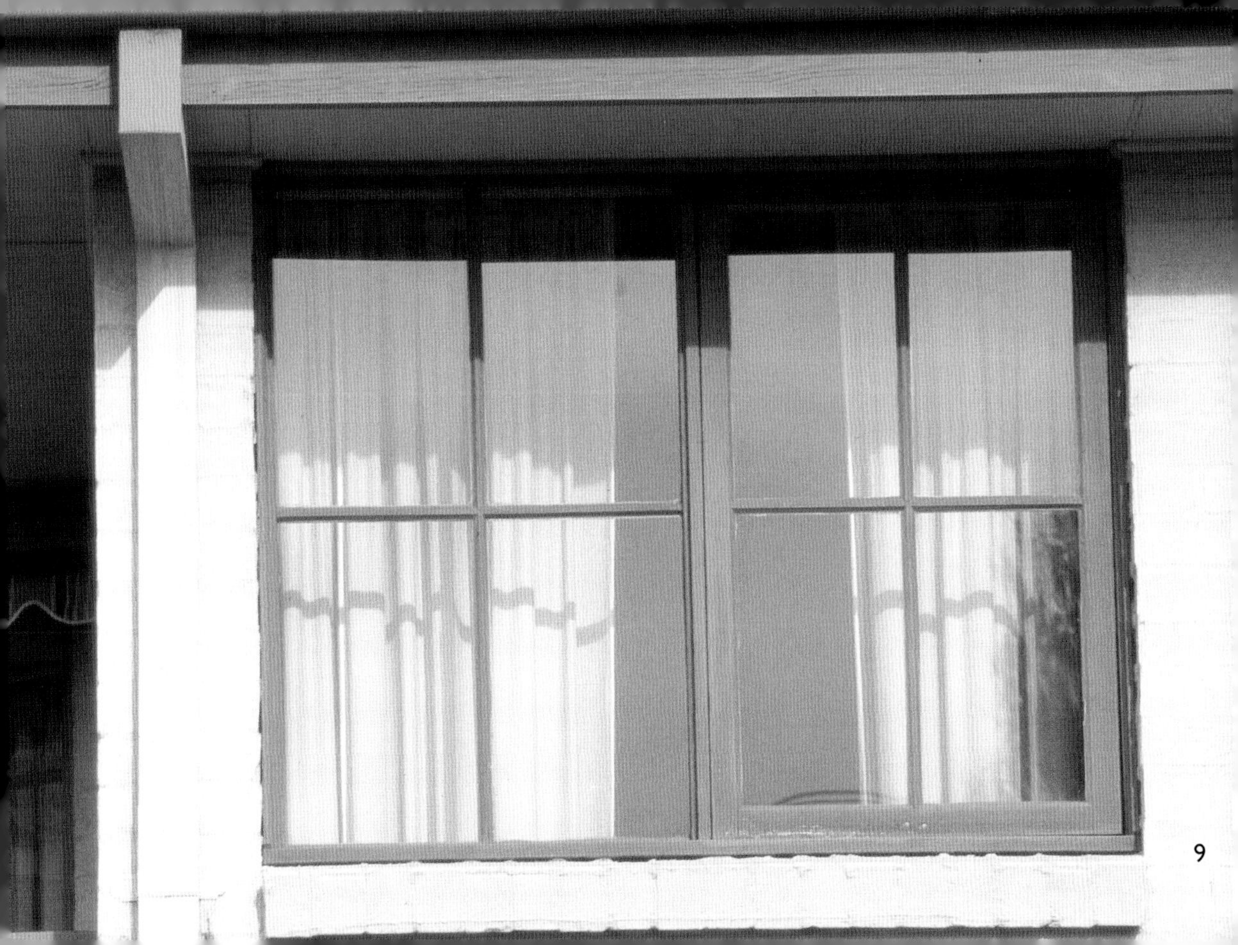

Here is a roof.

Here is a chimney.

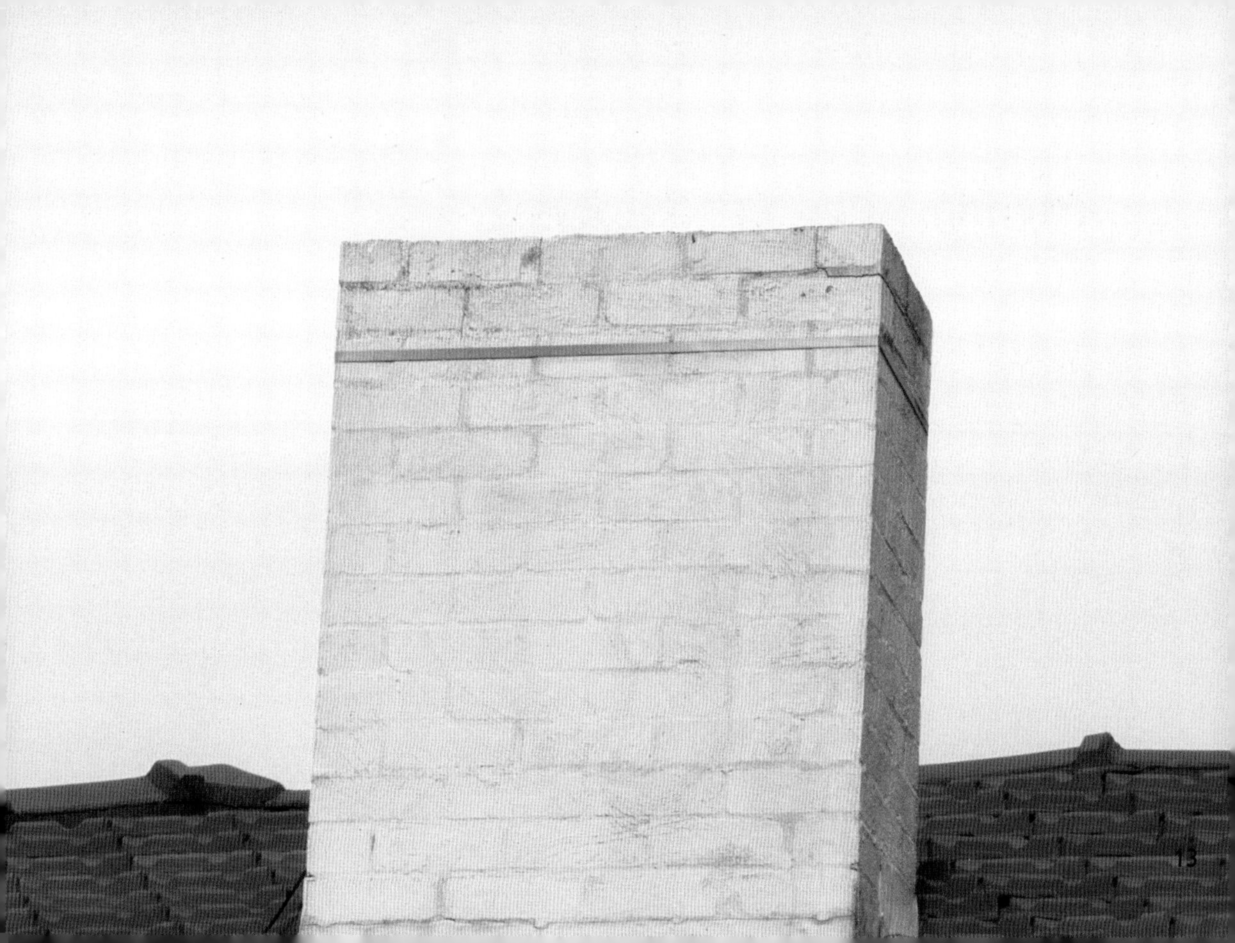

Here is a house.

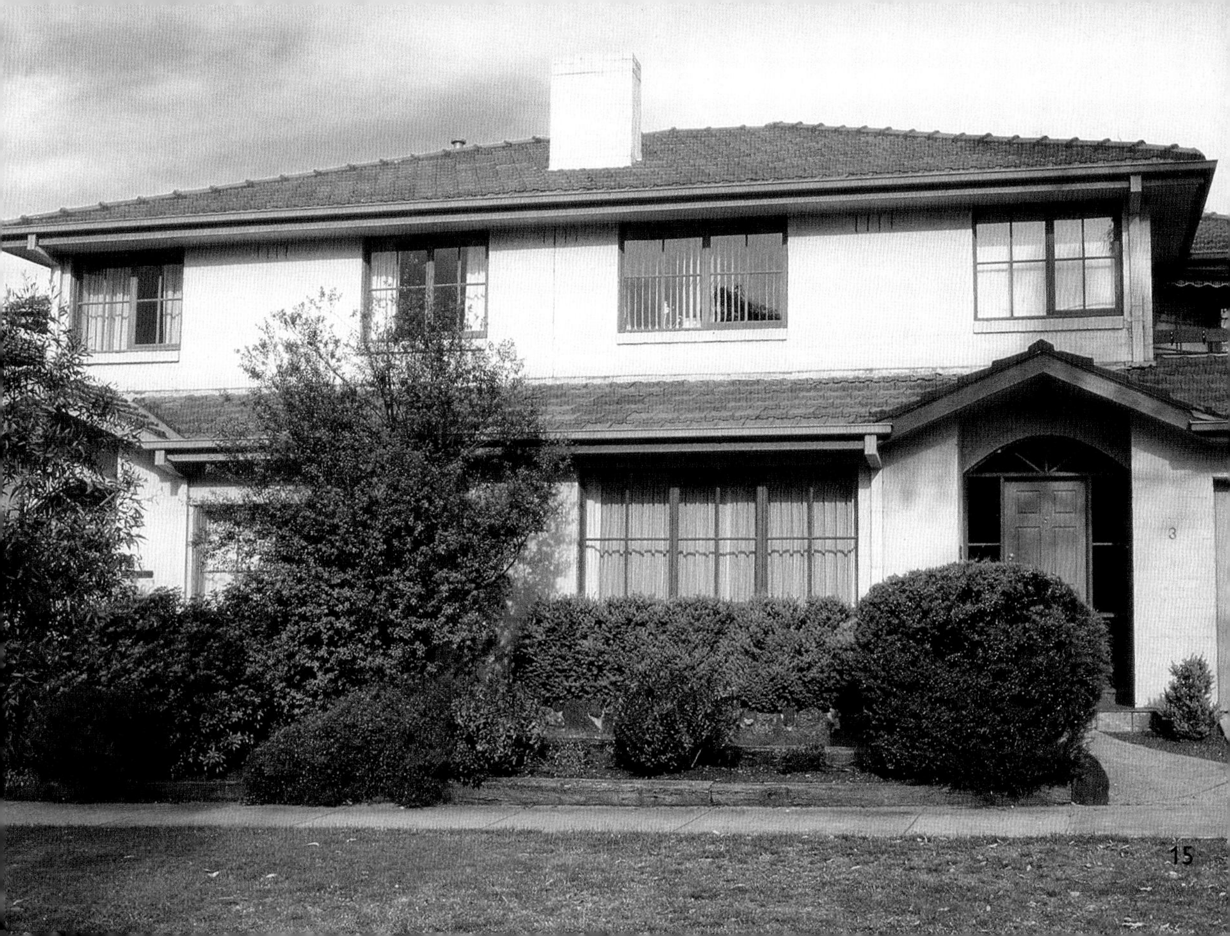
3

Here is a garden.

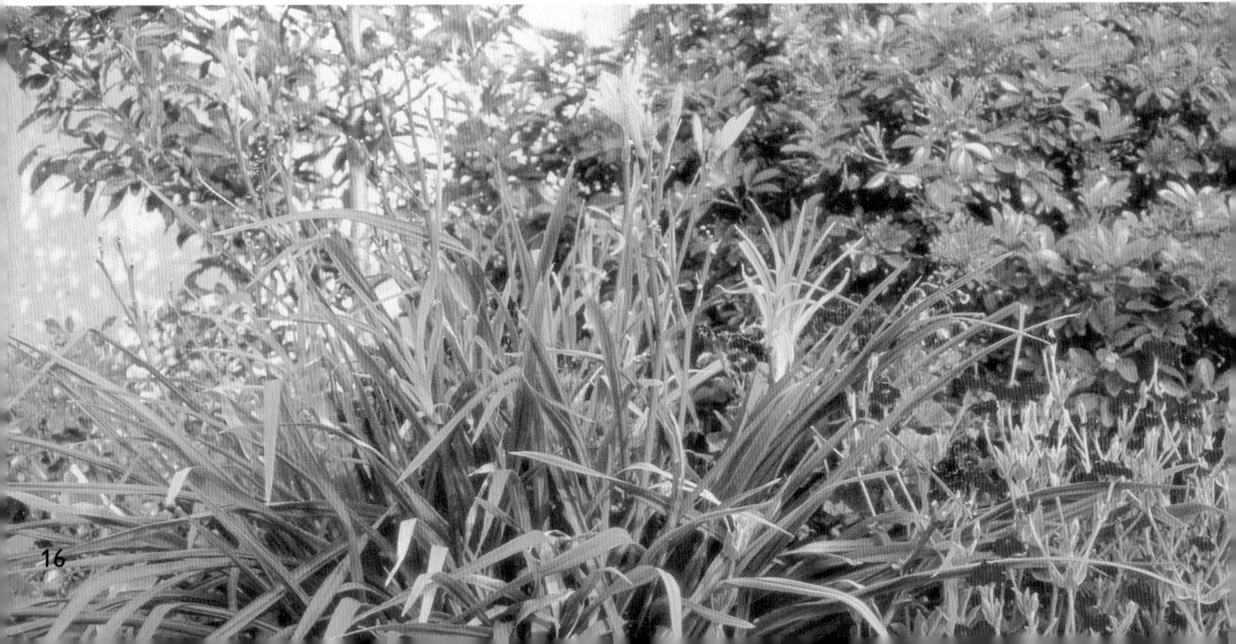